WHEN

**A holidaymaker's guide to the
language and the country**

Bob Powell

Producers
David Cordingley
Mick Webb

BBC BOOKS

This book accompanies the BBC television series
When in Italy, first broadcast on BBC 1 from April
1989 (produced by David Cordingley), and the radio
series of the same name, first broadcast on Radio 4
from April 1989 (produced by Mick Webb).

Published to accompany a series of programmes
prepared in consultation with the BBC Educational
Broadcasting Council.

BARNABY'S PICTURE LIBRARY (Gerald Clyde)
page 5; ROBERT HARDING front cover; BOB
POWELL page 36; MICK WEBB page 32.

The remaining photographs were taken for the BBC
by Brian Read.

© The Author and BBC Enterprises Limited 1989
First published 1989

Published by BBC Books, a division of BBC
Enterprises Ltd, Woodlands, 80 Wood Lane,
London W12 0TT

ISBN 0 563 21446 5

This book is set in 9 on 10½ point Century
Schoolbook

Printed in England by
Belmont Press, Northampton
Cover printed by Fletchers of Norwich, England.

CONTENTS

ABOUT THIS BOOK

- It's for people who are planning to go to Italy on holiday and would like to know something about the country, the people and the language.
- It can be used as a phrase book, or can be followed alongside the BBC tv and radio series *When in Italy*.
- The 15 sections are called **progetti** (plans). They cover the most common holiday situations, giving background information and useful phrases.
- There are exercises throughout and there's a reference section at the back with a basic grammar, an Italian to English vocabulary and wordlists to help with shopping, travelling, eating out and in emergencies.

HOW TO USE IT

- The **progetti** can be used in any order or you can work your way through the book from the beginning.
- For each **progetto**, read the introductory note and spend a few moments studying the key phrases.
- Read **action**, especially the parts of the conversation marked *You*. There's a pronunciation guide on page 9 with advice on getting the sounds right. Even better, listen to the recordings of these dialogues on the *When in Italy* cassette.
- Read the **replay** notes which explain a bit about how the language works, have a go at the **wordquiz** and when you have read the **factsheet**, do the **workout** exercises. Answers are at the back of the book.

WHEN IN ITALY CASSETTE

A C90 audio cassette is available as part of the *When in Italy* package. Listen to the conversations spoken by native speakers in Italy. There are also tips on pronunciation, words of guidance on using the essential phrases, and plenty of practice opportunities.

A few 'Don'ts'

Don't be embarrassed, have a go!
Most Italians you speak to will make every effort to help you learn their language.

Don't count your mistakes!
Getting the message over is what counts.

Don't be disappointed!
You won't remember every word the first time you see or hear it. Re-reading and repetition will help the words slip into your memory bank!

Buon viaggio . . . e coraggio!

ITALY AND THE ITALIANS

SOME FACTS AND FIGURES

- Italy has a surface area of over 300 000 square kilometres (116 350 square miles), about the same as the UK. The population (56 million) is also similar but the birth rate is declining sharply in some areas.

- Italy has frontiers with four other countries: France, Switzerland, Austria and Yugoslavia.

- Italy is divided into 20 regions, each with its own capital. These regions are, in their turn, subdivided into provinces. There are 94 of these altogether.

- Italy has only been a united nation for a little more than a century. Before 1870 there were several separate kingdoms and parts of the territory were under the control of foreign powers.

- Italy has been a republic since 1946, when the last king, Umberto II, abdicated following a referendum.

- Italy changes its government more frequently than many countries. There have been more than 40 since 1945.

- Italy was one of the founder states of the European Economic Community. The Treaty of Rome, which marked its creation, was signed in 1957.

- Italy's currency is the **lira**. But its value is due for a change. At the time this book was published, a 1000-lire bank note would not buy you much more than an espresso coffee. There are plans, however, to knock three zeros off the price of everything.

ITALIAN CITIES

Italy is now one of the world's richest countries, but the wealth of the nation is unevenly spread. The standard of living in the North is generally high, especially in and around Genoa, Milan and Turin. These three cities make up what is known as **il Triangolo Industriale**. Genoa is an important naval and commercial port, Turin is the home of the car manufacturing giant *Fiat*, and Milan is a

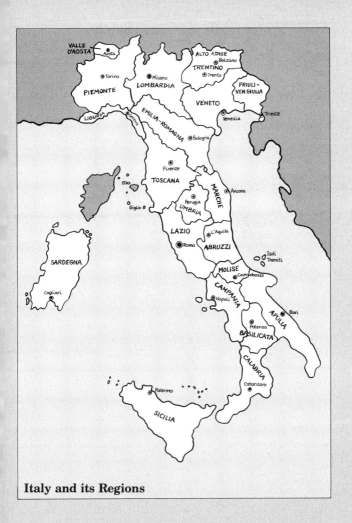

Italy and its Regions

7

financial centre as well as a world leader in fashion and design. Rome is, of course, the administrative capital and along with Florence and Venice the most popular destination for tourists. South of Rome, agriculture is the main source of income. In some parts the arid climate and unproductive soil make it hard to make a living and, over the years, many people from Naples and the rest of the South have headed to the northern cities in search of work. Many others have emigrated to the USA, Latin America and other European countries.

INSIDE ITALY, BUT NOT ITALIAN

Home of the Pope, the Vatican is not actually part of Italy but a separate state, with its own police force, coins, stamps and radio service.

If you are on holiday on the Adriatic coast, don't miss a trip to San Marino. This is another tiny area of the peninsula which is not Italian soil. It is the world's smallest republic with only 22 000 inhabitants. But over three million visitors cross the frontier every year.

ISLANDS

Italy has many islands. The largest of these is Sicily, whose capital, Palermo, is actually nearer Tunis in North Africa than Rome.

Sardinia harbours many prehistoric remains, and its Costa Smeralda (the 'Emerald Coast') is a favourite haunt of millionaires and jet-setters.

Particularly loved by the British are Ischia and Capri, and further north, off the Tuscan coast, is the island of Elba, where Napoleon I was exiled in 1817.

THE ITALIAN LANGUAGE

Modern Italian (**l'italiano**) is really a form of Tuscan dialect that was adopted as the national language during the last century. Many other dialects are spoken but the spread of education and modern communications, especially radio and tv, have made sure that virtually everyone you meet in Italy will speak Italian.

Don't forget that Italian is also one of the three official languages of neighbouring Switzerland. In the Ticino canton, at the north end of Lake Maggiore, Italian is the main language spoken.

LETTERS AND SOUNDS

Italian has a reputation for being a musical language and there's a very noticeable sing-song pattern to sentences. Most of the individual sounds are fairly straightforward, though the **g**'s and **c**'s sometimes cause difficulty for English speakers. Here is a rough guide to pronunciation:

a	'a' as in 'pat' not 'party' **pianta** (map)
ce and **ci**	'ch' as in 'church' **centro città** (city centre)
ch	'k' as in 'kite' **Che numero?** (What number?)
e	'e' as in 'Fred' **freddo** (cold)
ge and **gi**	'g' as in 'gin' **progetto** (project or plan) **vigile** (policeman)
gia, gio and **giu**	usually only the second vowel sound is pronounced **spiaggia** (beach) **giorno** (day) **laggiù** (down there)
gh	'g' as in 'ghetto' **traghetto** (ferry)

gli	'lli' as in 'million' **biglietto** (ticket)
h	not pronounced! **Ha . . . ?** (Do you have . . . ?)
i	'ee' as in 'feet' **indirizzo** (address)
o	'o' as in 'pot' **un po'** (a little)
qu	'qu' as in 'question' **quale?** (which?), **questo** (this), **qui** (here)
r	'r' is rolled by flicking the end of the tongue upwards as you say the words. **frutta e verdura** (fruit and vegetables)
s	's' has two sounds: 's' as in 'seen' **sinistra** (left) 'z' as in close' **chiuso** (closed) (It has the 'z' sound when it is between two vowels.)
sc	'sh' as in 'sugar' when followed by 'e' or 'i' **ascensore** (lift), **sciare** (to ski) 'sk' when followed by 'a', 'o' or 'u' **scatola** (box), **disco** (disk), **scusi** (excuse me)
u	'oo' as in 'mooing' **l'uva** (grapes)
z	'z' has two sounds: 'ts' as in 'cats' **piazza** (square) 'ds' as in 'suds' **mezzo** (half)

Most words are stressed on the last but one syllable:
posto   turismo   ristorante   arrivederci
A written accent on the last syllable shows where to stress the word.
caffè   città   così

Double consonants make a difference to the sound of a word. Linger longer over double letters, especially if they form part of the stressed syllable: **belli**s**simo** (very beautiful), **macchina** (car)

Your basic starter pack
Learn these essential words and phrases before you go any further! You can hear them at the beginning of the cassette.

1 Hello and goodbye

buongiorno	good morning, hello
buonasera	good evening, hello
buonanotte	good night
arrivederci	goodbye
ciao	see you *also* hi there

2 Yes and no

sì . . .no	yes . . .no

3 Being polite

per favore	please
grazie	thank you
prego	don't mention it
scusi	excuse me

4 Addressing people

signore	sir (Mr)
signora	madam (Mrs)
signorina	miss (Miss)

5 Numbers

1	**uno**	6	**sei**	
2	**due**	7	**sette**	
3	**tre**	8	**otto**	
4	**quattro**	9	**nove**	
5	**cinque**	10	**dieci**	

BUYING DRINKS

WHEN IN ITALY . . .
An Italian café is open to people of all ages from early
morning to very late at night. In some cafés you go
straight up to the counter and ask for your drink. In
others, you pay first at the cash-desk (**la cassa**) and then
take your receipt (**lo scontrino**) to the bar.

• Name your drink and add 'please':
Un caffè (a small black coffee)
Un caffelatte (a milky coffee)
Un tè (a tea)   } +**per favore.**
Una birra (a beer)
Un'aranciata (a fizzy orangeade)

• Asking the price – at the bar or the cash-desk:
Quant'è? (how much is it?)

• Understanding the prices:
mille lire (1000 lire)
duemila lire or just **duemila** (2000 lire)
tremilacinque lire (3500 lire)

ACTION You can hear these conversations on cassette side A.
You order a coffee at the bar of a café.

Signora	**Dica.**
You	**Un caffè, per favore.**
Signora	**Un espresso? Subito . . . ecco il caffè.**
You	**Grazie.**
Signora	**Prego.**

You pay for a beer and an orangeade at the cash-desk.

You	**Una birra, per favore.**
Cashier	**Duemila.**
You	**E un'aranciata, quant'è?**
Cashier	**Allora, millecinque, duemila:** **tremilacinque.**
You	**Ecco.**

At breakfast, you order a white coffee for yourself and a hot chocolate for your companion.

Waitress	**Buongiorno.**
You	**Buongiorno.**
Waitress	**Prendete il tè?**
You	**No. Un caffelatte e una cioccolata calda.**

At a café-terrace you order two beers and two lemon crushed-ice drinks.

You	**Scusi.**
Waitress	**Buonasera. Mi dica.**
You	**Due birre e due granite per favore.**
Waitress	**Le granite all'arancia o al limone?**
You	**Al limone.**
Waitress	**Sì, subito.**

REPLAY

1 If you have to attract someone's attention **scusi** (excuse me) is the word to use. The barman shows he is ready to serve you by saying **dica** or **mi dica**. When you have ordered, you may hear **subito** (immediately) as a sort of promise of fast service.

2 When you have to hand over cash, the little word **ecco** (here you are) can be used.

3 **Un caffè** can mean both *a* coffee and *one* coffee, just as **una birra** is *a* beer or *one* beer. Learn the appropriate word for 'a' each time you meet a new word. (There's more help on this and other grammar points on pages 73-76.)

4 When talking about more than one thing in Italian the last letter of a word tends to change: **una birra** but **due birre**; **un cappuccino** but **due cappuccini**. (See pages 73-74 for help with this too.) Don't let these changes in word endings worry you. After all it's the *number* of drinks that count.

5 If you don't catch the price, you can always check by looking at the receipt or asking for the amount to be written down. Say: **me lo scriva, per favore.** The *When in Italy* cassette gives practice in listening to numbers and prices.

WORDQUIZ

1 *Unscramble:* These jumbled words conceal three drinks. What are they?

a **caleafteft**   b **caniatara**   c **calcocatio**

2 *Doubling up:* Double the numbers of the drinks in these orders. Then read them aloud three times each. (Look at page 84 for help with numbers.)

a **un tè e un cappuccino**
b **una birra e tre granite**
c **due caffè e un'aranciata**

3 *Attention please:* You want to attract the barman's attention. Which of these words will work best?

a **ecco**   b **prego**   c **scusi**   d **grazie**

FACTSHEET 1: REFRESHMENTS – ITALIAN STYLE

Italians tend to take their light refreshments standing at the bar (**al bar**). If there are tables and chairs they will most likely be outside on the pavement area, and if you sit at a table (**al tavolo**) you will be charged more for the service.

Coffee and tea

Italians take their **espresso** coffee very strong, just a tiny cupful. If you want it a bit weaker ask for **un caffè lungo,** or stick to **cappuccino**, a frothy white coffee topped with chocolate powder. Tea is usually served with lemon (**al limone**) unless you make a point of asking for it with milk (**al latte**). Iced coffee (**caffè freddo**) is a treat on a hot day.

Beer

Italians drink mostly light, lager type beers. Unless you specially ask for a draught beer (**una birra alla spina**), you'll be served it bottled (**in bottiglia**) or from a can (**in lattina**).

Soft drinks

A bottled fruit juice is **un succo di frutta** but for one prepared on the spot from fresh fruit ask for **una spremuta**. **Granite** are crushed-ice drinks.

WORKOUT

1 It's breakfast time and the waitress asks whether you want coffee. You would prefer tea with milk. How would you reply?

2 At the end of a meal you order coffee for yourself and your friend. What do you say?

3 At the beach snack-bar, you have a large order for drinks for the family and friends. A beer for yourself, two orangeades, and four crushed-ice drinks, all lemon flavour. Can you cope with the order?

4 You are asked how you like your beer. You would really prefer draught if they have it. Which of these do you say?

a **in lattina**   b **alla spina**   c **in bottiglia**

GETTING INFORMATION

WHEN IN ITALY . . .

Every region has its Tourist Board Office (**Ente Provinciale Turismo**) in the regional capital. But many other towns, certainly the holiday centres, have their own offices too. These are known by the grand title of **Azienda Autonoma di Soggiorno e Turismo**.

● To find out whether there is a local tourist office in the town, the simplest question is:

C'è un ufficio turismo qui?

● Asking when a place is open:

Quando è aperto?

● Asking for a town plan:

Una pianta della città, per favore.

● Getting a list of hotels and restaurants:

Ha un listino alberghi e ristoranti?

16

ACTION You can hear these conversations on cassette side A.

Asking where the tourist information office is located.

You　　　**Scusi, c'è un ufficio turismo qui?**
Signorina **Sì. In centro città, in Piazza Garibaldi.**
You　　　**Piazza Garibaldi. Grazie.**
Signorina **Prego.**

The office is just closing for lunch. You are told it opens
again at four o'clock.

Clerk　　**Mi dispiace, ma è chiuso.**
You　　　**Quando è aperto?**
Clerk　　**Alle quattro.**

At the tourist office, asking for a street map of the town and a list of hotels and restaurants.

You	**Una pianta della città, per favore.**
Clerk	**Sì, certo. Eccola. Desidera altro?**
You	**Sì. Ha un listino alberghi e ristoranti?**
Clerk	**Sì. Eccolo.**

You also ask about the local festival and pick up a brochure.

You	**Ha informazioni sulla festa?**
Clerk	**Sì. In inglese? (Sì) Ecco un dépliant.**

REPLAY

1 There are several words for 'the': **il**, **la**, **lo** and, in front of words beginning with a vowel, **l'**. See page 73-74 for advice on which one to use.

2 Written with an accent **è** means 'is'. Without an accent, it means 'and'. They both sound the same. **C'è** means 'there is', and said with a questioning tone 'is there?'

3 When checking on what is available, you can also use the little word **ha** meaning 'do you have?' Remember not to pronounce the 'h'.

4 Giuseppe Garibaldi is a national hero. He fought to unite Italy as one nation during the nineteenth century. Virtually every Italian town has a Garibaldi Square.

5 Desidera altro? is one way people will ask you whether you need anything else.

WORDQUIZ

1 *Watch your p's:* Unjumble these four words and give the English meanings. Tip: they all begin with a 'p' in Italian.

a **zipaz**   b **grope**   c **zapiza**   d **panati**

2 *Odd one out:* Which is the odd one out in this set?

a **albergo**   b **dépliant**   c **ristorante**   d **ufficio**

3 *Open and shut:* Which of these signs would you prefer to see on a bank door?

a **chiuso**   b **aperto**

FACTSHEET 2: FINANCE & FESTIVALS

Changing money

Some of the more important tourist offices have an exchange counter (**cambio**) where you can change your traveller's cheques or cash. The British pound is known as **la sterlina**. Some hotels will change money, too, but you will probably get a better deal at a bank (**una banca**). You will probably be asked for your address (**il suo indirizzo**) and your signature (**la sua firma**) on the dotted line before you are sent to a central cash-desk to pick up your money. Banking hours are 8.30am to 1.30pm and 2.45pm to 3.45pm, Monday to Friday. There are also privately run **Uffici Cambio** which are open longer hours and on Saturdays.

Festivals

In most Italian towns and villages people celebrate their local saint's day with **una festa**. In some places you'll come across another kind of festival called **una sagra**, in honour of an important local crop or product e.g. in Perugia there's **la sagra della castagna** (the feast of the chestnut). During the summer, the Communist Party also organises local celebrations called **la festa dell'Unità.**

WORKOUT
1 You've just arrived in a village. How would you ask if there's an information office?
2 There is probably a map of the town at the newspaper kiosk. How would you check whether the man has one?
3 In a seaside resort, the camp site where you hoped to stay is full. At the tourist office, ask for a list of camp sites (**campeggi**).
4 Ask whether there is a bank in the town.
5 At the end of a long list of enquiries you are asked: **Desidera altro?** Say 'No thanks' and 'Goodbye'.

1 Ciao! ('Hi!')

2 Non lo so. ('I don't know.')

3 Beve? ('Like a drink?')

4 Va via! ('Go away!')

5 Che vuoi? ('What do you want?')

MAKING CONTACT

WHEN IN ITALY . . .
It's absolutely true that Italians love talking – with
plenty of gestures, of course. And you can be sure that it
won't be long before you find yourself drawn into a
conversation and need to say something about yourself.

- Giving your name:
Mi chiamo . . . (My name is . . .)

- Stating your nationality:
Sono inglese/scozzese/gallese/irlandese.
(I am English/Scottish/Welsh/Irish.)

- Saying where you come from:
Sono di Londra. (I am from London.)

- Saying where you are staying:
Sto all'hotel . . . (I am staying at the hotel. . .)

ACTION

ACTION You can hear these conversations on cassette side A.

You are sharing a dinner table with a friendly-looking
Italian woman. You ask her name.

You **Lei, come si chiama?**
Signora **Mi chiamo Elena. E lei?**
You **Mi chiamo Denise.**

She asks you if you're on holiday.

Elena **Lei è in vacanza?**
You **Sì, sto all'Hotel della Posta.**

She finds out a little more about you.

Elena **Lei è inglese?**
You **Sì, sono inglese.**
Elena **E di Londra?**
You **No. Sono di Cambridge.**

You ask whether she lives locally.

You **Lei è di qui?**
Elena **No, non sono di qui. Sono di Roma. Sono
romana.**

REPLAY
1 **Lei** is one word for 'you'. It's used when talking to
strangers, or to adults you don't know very well. When
you're on friendly terms with someone, you're more likely
to use **tu**. Both **tu** and **lei** are often left out, e.g. **è di
Londra?**
2 Asking an adult's name is **come si chiama?** To a child
you say **come ti chiami?** Remember that the **ch** in **mi
chiamo** is a hard sound like a 'k'.
3 **Di** is a versatile word. It can mean both 'of' and 'from'.
4 **Sono** is 'I am'; **non sono** is 'I am not'. The word for 'I' is
'**io**' though it's often not used.

WORDQUIZ
1 *Roots:* Fill in the gaps to show these people's national
identity.

a **Mi chiamo Bob. Sono di Londra. Sono** . . . . . . **ese.**
b **Mi chiamo Joyce. Sono di Glasgow. Sono** . . . . . .
ese.
c **Mi chiamo Liam. Sono di Dublin. Sono** . . . . . . **ese.**

22

2 *City links:* Five Italian cities are hidden in this chain. Can you identify them? They are the Italian names, not the English versions of them. (If you get stuck, look at the map on page 7.)

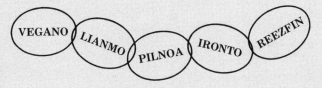

FACTSHEET 3: ITALIAN ORIGINS

The number-plates of Italian vehicles indicate clearly where they come from. Apart from Rome (ROMA) which is written in full, each province has a two-letter code which comes before the actual number.

Here are the names of some of the main Italian towns together with the abbreviated code. The words in the last column are used to describe people or things coming from those towns. They are found a lot in menus to describe types of sauces or styles of cooking.

Bologna (BO) (Bologna) **bolognese**
Firenze (FI) (Florence) **fiorentino**
Genova (GE) (Genoa) **genovese**
Napoli (NA) (Naples) **napoletano**
Torino (TO) (Turin) **torinese**
Venezia (VE) (Venice) **veneziano**

WORKOUT

1 You decide to find out the name of the hotel waiter who is serving you regularly. What is the question you should ask?
2 Ask him whether he is a local person.
3 He knows that you are English-speaking but assumes you come from London. How would you tell him: 'No, I am not from London. I am Welsh.'?
4 He asks you: **Come si chiama?** How would *you* reply?

WHICH LANGUAGE?

WHEN IN ITALY . . .
Until fairly recently French was the first foreign language
taught in schools. So quite a few people you meet may
have a smattering of French, if they don't understand
English.

● Asking someone which language he or she speaks:

Parla { **inglese?** (English)
{ **francese?** (French)

● Saying you don't understand or you haven't heard
properly:

Non capisco.
Come?

● Finding out the names of things:

Come si chiama questo?

ACTION You can hear these conversations on cassette side A.

You ask a woman the way to the Trevi fountain but her answer leaves you a bit bewildered.

You	**Per la Fontana di Trevi, per favore.**
Signora	**Dunque . . . bisogna prendere questa strada fino al semaforo e poi . . .**
You	**Scusi, non capisco.**

You have difficulty communicating with someone so you ask whether she speaks English – or French.

You	**Parla inglese?**
Signora	**No, mi dispiace, no.**
You	**Parla francese?**
Signora	**No. Parlo soltanto italiano.**

You are asked whether you speak Italian. You confess to speaking just a little bit.

Signora	**Parla italiano?**
You	**Sì, un pochino.**

At the market cheese stall you ask the name of a local speciality. You don't catch the name the first time.

You	**Come si chiama questo?**
Signora	**Provolone.**
You	**Come?**
Signora	**Si chiama provolone. Provolone molto buono.**

REPLAY

1 What the woman actually says is: 'You must take this street as far as the traffic lights and then . . .' (See Progetto 5 for help with directions.)

2 **Molto** means 'much', 'a lot', 'a great deal'. To say 'not a lot' just put a **non** in front of it, for example when telling the waiter you want only a small portion of spaghetti! **Molto** can also mean 'very' as in **molto buono** (very good).

3 The opposite of **molto** is **poco** (a little). This is usually shortened to **un po'**. **Un pochino**, though a longer word, actually means something even smaller, a tiny bit.

4 Use **parla inglese?** when speaking to adults. To a child you should say: **parli inglese?**

5 The simplest way to apologise politely is the phrase **mi dispiace**.

6 **Provolone** is a hard, strongly-flavoured, oval-shaped cheese.

WORDQUIZ

1 *Front to back:* Read these words aloud backwards, split them up where necessary and you should have three possible answers to the question: **Parla italiano?**

a **opnuis**   b **ecaipsidimon**

c **onailatiotlomolrapnonon**

2 *Coping with stress:* Listen to the conversations on the cassette, then underline the syllables which you should stress most.
The first one is done for you already.

a **Parla <u>in</u>glese?**

b **Parla italiano?**

c **Scusi, non capisco.**

d **Parlo soltanto italiano.**

e **Come si chiama questo?**

3 *I speak, you speak:* Only three of the following words really exist. Which are they, and which of them means 'I speak'?

parlese parla parlat parli parlu parlia parlo parle

FACTSHEET 4: THE LANGUAGES OF ITALY

Northern Italy has frontiers with four countries. Working from west to east they are: France (**La Francia**), Switzerland (**La Svizzera**), Austria (**L'Austria**) and Yugoslavia (**la Jugoslavia** – pronounced like the English word). The languages usually associated with these countries can also be found over the borders, in neighbouring parts of Italy. Don't be surprised to hear German (**il tedesco**) in the Dolomites, or French in the Aosta valley above Turin.

Sicily has a particular dialect (**il siciliano**) with traces of Greek and Arabic. Sardinians have their own distinctive language (**il sardo**), with many forms resembling the Latin spoken by the Romans two thousand years ago.

In many parts of the peninsula and on the islands that make up the Italian nation it is the local dialect that people learn first, with modern Italian second.

WORKOUT

1 The car-park attendant is trying to tell you something but you don't really understand very well. Which of the following could you say?

a **questo per favore**   b **non capisco**
c **molto buono**   d **un pochino**

2 You are comparing notes with a fellow traveller about the number of languages you speak. Say: 'I speak French a little. I don't speak much Italian.'

3 You want to know the name of the place you have just stopped at. How do you ask the guide? (The word for place is **posto**.)

4 Someone asks you: **Parla tedesco?** What do they want to know?

SIGHTSEEING BY BUS AND ON FOOT

WHEN IN ITALY . . .

Parking is a major problem in most Italian towns and cities. Even if you have driven all the way to Italy, it's not a bad idea to take a bus if you plan to see the sights. In some cities you can even catch a tram (**un tram**) or a trolleybus (**un filobus**) and in Rome and Milan there's the underground (**la Metropolitana**).

• Catching the right bus:

L'autobus per . . .? (plus the name of your destination)

• Asking where a place is:

Dov'è il Colosseo?

• Essential directions to listen out for:

a sinistra (left)
a destra (right)
dritto (straight on)

A bus stop (**fermata**).

Buying tickets (**biglietti**).

Badia di San Salvatore
(sec. XI)

PANTANO 15

31 PERUGIA

CORCIANO

ACTION You can hear these conversations on cassette side A.

In Rome, you ask a passer-by where to catch a bus to Piazza Navona.

You	**L'autobus per Piazza Navona, per favore?**
Signore	**La fermata è a sinistra, a centro metri.**
You	**Grazie. Che numero?**
Signore	**Sessantaquattro.**
You	**Sessantaquattro, grazie.**

On the bus, you check where to get off and push your way to the exit door.

You	**La fermata per Piazza Navona?**
Signora	**Questa o la prossima.**
You	**Grazie . . . scusi, permesso.**

You want to visit the Forum (**il foro romano**) but you're having trouble finding the way in.

You	**Dov'è l'entrata, per favore?**
Guide	**Sempre dritto e poi a destra.**
You	**Grazie. E lontano?**
Guide	**No. Non è lontano. E molto vicino . . . a due o trecento metri.**

REPLAY

1 Bus tickets (**biglietti**) must normally be bought in advance. You save money by buying a book of ten (**un blocchetto**) at a newspaper kiosk (**edicola**) or at a tobacconist's shop (**tabaccheria**) where you see the sign BIGLIETTIBUS. Don't forget the **gli** sound in **biglietti** (like the 'lli' in 'million'.)

2 Per usually means 'for', and is handy when you're asking the way: **per . . .** followed by the name of the street, town, building, monuments etc.

3 Number tips: To be sure that you have heard a price or set of numbers correctly, why not repeat them out loud? It will help you remember, too.

4 The next stop is **la prossima fermata**. The one after that will be **la seconda** (second) **fermata**, and after that **la terza** (third) **fermata**. You'll also hear these numbers when being directed to a street: **la prima strada** – the first street, **la seconda strada** etc.

5 As you make your way to the exit on the bus, say **permesso** as you squeeze past other passengers.

6 Dov'è? means 'Where is?'; **dove sono?** means 'where are?'

7 Vicino (near) is the opposite of **lontano** (far).

WORDQUIZ

1 *Number sequences:* Write down the Italian words for the numbers in these sequences. (Look at page 84 for assistance.)

a 3 - ......, 13 - ......, 33 - ......

b 5 - ......, 15 - ......, 55 - ......

c 8 - ......, 18 - ......, 88 - ......

2 *Pointing the way:*
Put the arrows in the correct boxes.

a	**a sinistra**
b	**dritto**
c	**a destra**

3 *Near and far:* Complete these sentences using either **vicino** or **lontano**.

a **Napoli è a 600km. E ......!**

b **La fontana di Trevi è ......, soltanto a centro metri.**

c **Piazza Garibaldi non è .... E qui in centro città.**

FACTSHEET 5: STREET NAMES

The most common word for a street is the old Latin word **via**. You can still walk along the Appian Way (**la via Appia**) in Rome. Some city streets are named after national heroes or famous statesmen such as Garibaldi, Cavour and Mazzini, and these crop up in virtually every place you go to. Other roads commemorate important dates in Italy's history. **Via XXV Aprile**, for example, recalls the Liberation of Italy from German occupation in 1945.

There are several words for a square. A broad, open square in front of a railway station may be called **piazzale,** whereas a narrower square at a road junction is likely to be called a **largo**. The main high street is often called **corso**, and a wide, tree-lined avenue is a **viale**. In the ancient parts of some towns you may walk down a narrow lane called a **vicolo**, and in Venice, signs of Spanish influence remain, literally, in the local word for 'street': **calle**.

WORKOUT

1 You want to catch the bus but you have run out of tickets. You pop into a bar near the bus stop and ask for a book of ten. What do you say?

2 You want to catch the bus to **via Magenta**. How do you find out which number bus to get on?

3 You are on the bus at last. The passenger next to you tells you: **Via Magenta è la terza fermata.** Do you get off after one, two or three stops?

4 Despite all the good advice, you manage to get off the bus at the wrong stop! You are wondering which way to walk. Stop someone and ask where **via Magenta** is.

A SNACK AND AN ICE CREAM

WHEN IN ITALY . . .

Touring around, sightseeing or even sitting on the beach can be hungry and thirsty work. But there's usually no shortage of places where you can get a light snack or one of those fruity-flavoured ice-creams that Italy is famous for.

● Things to order for a snack:

un panino (a roll)
un gelato (an ice-cream)   } **+ per favore**
un po' di pizza (a piece of pizza)

● Asking how much it costs: **Quanto costa?**

● Large or small?   **Grande o piccolo?**

kiwi   tiramisú   zuppa inglese

ACTION You can hear these conversations on cassette side A.

You buy two rolls filled with roast-pork (**porchetta**) at a
market stall.

You	**Due panini per favore.**
Signora	**Sì, subito . . . va bene così?**
You	**Sì. Quanto costa?**
Signora	**Duemila lire l'uno. Sono due. Quattromila.**
You	**Ecco quattromila lire.**

You buy a piece of pizza at a take-away pizzeria.

You	**Un po' di pizza, per favore.**
Signora	**Quale? Questa al pomodoro e mozzarella?**
You	**Sì.**
Signora	**Va bene così?**
You	**Sì, grazie, va bene.**

You cannot resist an ice-cream and you ask for three different flavours to fill your cone.

You	**Un gelato, per favore.**
Signore	**Grande o piccolo?**
You	**Grande.**
Signore	**Cosa preferisce? Fragola, nocciola, limone . . .**
You	**Fragola, limone e un po' di questo.**
Signore	**Allora, fragola, limone e pistacchio.**

REPLAY

1 The answer to **va bene così?** (is this okay?) can be quite simply **va bene** (it's fine).

2 Ice-creams come in cones of various sizes (**coni**), or tubs (**coppini**). There is no space to list here all the flavours (**i gusti**) available in Italy. Amongst the ones mentioned in this conversation were strawberry (**fragola**) and hazelnut (**nocciola**).

3 If you are asked to make a choice, the question will be **Quale?** or **Cosa preferisce?** You can start by saying **Preferisco** (I prefer), but if you don't know the name for something, don't get flustered, just point and ask for **un po' di questo** (a bit of this).

WORDQUIZ

1 *Number match:* Match up the words on the left with the correct number on the right.

a **millecinque**	i	4000
b **tremilaquattrocento**	ii	1500
c **seimilasettecentocinquanta**	iii	3400
d **quattromila**	iv	6750

2 *Mixed flavours:* Unscramble these ice-cream flavours.

a **facèf** b **nolemi**
c **iccalono** d **gloarfa**

FACTSHEET 6: WHERE TO GO FOR SNACKS
There seems to be a café on almost every corner,
and most of them stock a kind of sweet breakfast
roll known as **una brioche** (pronounced 'bree-osh')
or a croissant (**un cornetto**). The bar staff will also
make you a savoury toasted sandwich (**un toast**).
For a wider range of rolls or sandwiches
(**tramezzini**) try one of the newer sandwich bars
that go under the name of **paninoteca**.

Try real Italian ice-cream in a **gelateria** (ice-cream
parlour) or fancy cake, **una pasta**, in a
pasticceria. These two establishments are often
combined in one colourful, sweet-smelling shop,
open until late in the evening.

In a baker's shop (**panetteria, panificio** or **forno**),
you can get several different kinds of bread. But they
also bake and sell pizza of various types including
foccaccia, which is made with cheese (**formaggio**)
and sometimes with onion as well (**cipolla**). These
savoury snacks are usually sold by weight but you can
also ask for a specific amount in cash.

WORKOUT
1 You and a friend are feeling a bit hungry so you pop
into a **paninoteca** with a take-away counter. Take part
in this dialogue.

You	(Ask, politely, for two rolls.)
Signorina	**Cosa preferisce?**
You	(There's a choice of **porchetta** or **formaggio.** Ask for cheese.)
Signorina	**Subito.**
You	(Ask how much it costs.)
Signorina	**Duemila l'uno.**
You	(You hand over the money, saying the total price.)

2 You are not sure which ice-cream to choose so you
plump for the nicest colour and say: 'A bit of this, please'.
What's that in Italian?
3 The ice-cream maker is concocting a complicated dish
with fruit and cream topping. How would you ask him
what it is called?

SHOPPING FOR A PICNIC

WHEN IN ITALY . . .
Although the idea of shopping in a large supermarket (**un supermercato**) is catching on rapidly, Italians still seem to prefer the friendly atmosphere of the small, all-purpose family grocer's shop. The **alimentari** will supply almost everything you need for a picnic.

● Begin your shopping list by saying **Mi dà . . .** (Give me)

● To ask for a precise amount:
quattro fette di prosciutto (four slices of ham)

● Asking for items by weight or volume:
un chilo di pomodori (a kilo of tomatoes)
un litro di vino rosso (a litre of red wine)

● Or, more vaguely:
un po' d'uva (a few grapes)

+ **per favore.**

● Saying 'that's enough':
Basta così.

ACTION You can hear these conversations on cassette side A.

You buy four slices of ham and some mild cheese at the corner shop.

You	**Questo prosciutto, per favore.**
Signora	**Quanto ne vuole?**
You	**Quattro fette.**
Signora	**Poi?**
You	**Un po' di formaggio.**
Signora	**Questo è dolce. Va bene?**
You	**Sì. Due etti, per favore.**

You want a kilo of tomatoes and a few grapes.

You	**Un chilo di pomodori, per favore.**
Signora	**Sì, subito. Che altro vuole?**
You	**Un po' d'uva.**
Signora	**Subito. Va bene così?**
You	**Sì, va bene. Grazie.**

And to wash it down, mineral water and red wine.

Signora	**Vuole altro?**
You	**Mi dà una bottiglia d'acqua minerale e questa bottiglia di vino.**
Signora	**Nient'altro?**
You	**No, basta così, grazie.**

REPLAY

1 When you are asked **quanto ne vuole?** get ready to say the amount you want.

2 Slices (**fette**) of ham can be cooked (**cotto**) or cured (**crudo**).

3 Cheese can be mild (**dolce**), mature (**stagionato**) or even spicy (**piccante**).

4 100 grams is **un etto**, 200 grams (about seven ounces) is **due etti**. 500 grams can be **cinquecento grammi** or **mezzo chilo**. Remember that a kilogram (**un chilo**) is about 2.2lb in weight.

5 The word **di** (of) comes in for a lot of use with weights and quantities. It is shortened to **d'** in front of words beginning with a vowel.

6 If you want a bit more cheese or a few more tomatoes the phrase to use is **un po' di più**. 'A bit less' is **un po' di meno**. When the quantity is just right, you can say: **va bene così** (that's okay) or **basta così** (that's enough).

WORDQUIZ

1 *Weight-watching:* Match the figure on the left with the correct phrase on the right. Practise saying them out loud.

a	½kg	i	**un etto**
b	200g	ii	**mezzo chilo**
c	1kg	iii	**due etti**
d	100g	iv	**un chilo**

2 *Anything else?* Which of these phrases might a shopkeeper use to ask whether you want anything else? Hint: There could be more than one answer here.

a **vuole altro?** b **e poi?** c **nient'altro?** d **basta così?**

FACTSHEET 7: SHOPPING FOR FOOD

Buying bread

All bread is sold by weight, even small rolls. You can get it in many general food stores, **alimentari,** as well as baker's shops.

Buying meat

For fresh meat, go to a **macelleria**. No large shop windows here. Just a little door with a screen to stop the flies entering and a cool, marble-slabbed interior. Indeed, in the summer, do not expect to find much meat on display. Common cuts of meat are **cotolette** (slices for frying) and **braciole** (chops).

If you are keen on cooked meats, **salami**, ham and so on, look for a **salumeria**. For poultry, you may sometimes see a specialist shop called a **polleria**.

Buying fruit and vegetables

Most Italian towns have a weekly open-air market (**un mercato**) and this is probably the best place to buy perishable goods. The market has an atmosphere of its own and prices are very competitive.

WORKOUT

1 Bearing in mind that peaches are **pesche** and apples are **mele**, how would you ask for these items on the shopping list for your picnic?

1kg peaches	5 slices of ham
200g cheese	½kg tomatoes
10 bread rolls	5 apples

2 Having asked for 200g of cheese, you suddenly decide that you would like a little more. What do you say?

3 You get to the end of the order and the shopkeeper asks you: **Nient'altro?** What do you reply?

4 Ask how much it all comes to.

5 You are told: **quattordicimilasettecentocinquanta lire.** How much change do you get out of 15 000 lire?

SHOPPING FOR PRESENTS AND POSTCARDS

WHEN IN ITALY . . .

Italy, famous for its style in most things, offers a wide range of handmade goods to take home as souvenirs or presents: glass, leather, lace etc. Postcards and stamps are best bought together at the tobacconist's shop, to avoid queues at the post office (**la posta**). Look for the sign with the white 'T' on a blue background.

• Saying the number of cards you have chosen:
dieci cartoline

• Asking for stamps:
Ha francobolli?

• Asking to try something on:
Posso provare questo?

• Saying something is very nice . . .
E molto bello . . .
E bellissimo . . .

• Turning something down:
No. Grazie.

ACTION You can hear these conversations on cassette side B.

You stock up with postcards at the gift shop, and you're in luck – they sell stamps there too.

You	**Dieci cartoline.**
Signora	**Dieci cartoline a duecento lire. Duemila lire.**
You	**Ha francobolli per la Gran Bretagna?**
Signora	**Sì, per tutte e dieci le cartoline?**
You	**Sì.**

You ask to try on a leather jacket in the market but decide not to buy.

You	**Posso provare questa giacca?**
Signora	**Che taglia?**
You	**Quarantadue.**
Signora	**Ecco il numero quarantadue. Va bene?**
You	**No . . . è troppo piccola.**
Signora	**Questa è più grande. Va bene?**
You	**No, grazie.**

You find some beautiful lacework, but it's a bit expensive

for you. You are lucky to get a reduction without really
asking.

You	**Quanto costa, signora?**
Signora	**Trentacinquemila. E molto bello, no? Le piace?**
You	**Sì, è bellissimo. Ma troppo caro.**
Signora	**Guardi, signore, facciamo trentamila lire. Va bene?**
You	**Trentamila lire. Sì, va bene. Grazie.**

REPLAY

1 When asking permission to do something, e.g. smoke,
open a window, try on clothes, start by saying **posso?**
People will generally understand what you want,
especially if you point or make an appropriate gesture!
2 If something is too expensive, say **troppo caro**, and
you might get a discount, **uno sconto**.
3 To say you like something is **mi piace**. If you don't like
it, **non mi piace. Mi dispiace,** on the other hand, means
'I'm sorry'.

WORDQUIZ

1 *Do your sums:* If postcards cost **cinquecento lire
l'una**, what do the following cost? Write down the
numbers in figures *and* words.

a **tre cartoline**   b **quattro cartoline**
c **otto cartoline**   d **dieci cartoline**

2 *Missing vowels:* Fill in the missing vowels and then
re-arrange the words to make sentences.

a c_r_ _ m_ tr_pp_ b_ll_ss_m_
b q__st_ p_ss_ pr_v_r_?
c fr_nc_b_ll_ h_ c_rt_l_n_ p_r?

3 *Boxed in:* Start with an 'M' and by following different
routes, you should come up with the Italian for 'I'm sorry,
I don't like it'.

a					b					c				
I	D	I	M		E	C	A	I	P		I	S	O	N	E
A	I	P	S		I	M	N	O	N		D	P	N	M	C
O	N	E	C		E	C	A	I	P		I	I	E	I	A
P	I	M	N		S	I	D	I	M		M	A	C	P	I
E	C	A	I												

FACTSHEET 8: MADE IN ITALY

Italian fashion designers such as Armani, Krizia, Missoni and Versace are famous throughout the world. Prices for their knitwear, suits and dresses are naturally out of the reach of many people. However, large chain stores such as Standa, Coin and Upim offer some stylish goods at more affordable prices. Look out for the special offer (**promozione**) at the time of the sales (**saldi**). Price tags will show the percentage reductions, e.g. **sconto – 15%**.

Traditional Italian crafts (**l'artigianato**) include leather work in Florence, and glass-blowing on the Venetian island of Murano. In Naples you can buy **terracotta** statuettes, Sorrento is famous for its marquetry, and working in lace (**il pizzo**) still provides people with a living, as you'll find in many popular holiday resorts.

WORKOUT

1 You have bought some postcards in a little shop but you want to check whether they sell stamps. What do you say?

2 The hat (**cappello**) you try on is too big. Ask politely for a smaller size.

3 You pick up a pullover in the market and there's no size label on it. How would you ask to try it on?

4 It fits! So you ask how much it is.

5 An Italian friend thinks it looks really nice on you. Which of these phrases could she say? (Hint: more than one.)

a **troppo grande** b **è molto bello**
c **non va bene** d **mi piace**

GETTING SOMEWHERE TO STAY

WHEN IN ITALY . . .
Checking into a hotel or camp site is not a complicated operation and a few simple phrases will soon get you a roof over your head. If you can book in advance, the process is even smoother.

● Asking whether there is space at the camp site . . .
C'è posto?

● . . . or a room in the hotel:
Ha una camera?

● Understanding what rooms are available:
una singola con doccia (a single room with a shower)
una doppia con bagno (a double with private bathroom)

● To say you have a reservation:
Ho una prenotazione.

ACTION You can hear these conversations on cassette side B.
You book your family into a camp site.

You	**Buonasera. C'è posto?**
Signore	**Per una tenda?**
You	**Sì.**
Signore	**Per quante persone?**
You	**Due adulti e due bambini.**

You arrive at the hotel where you have previously booked a single room with a shower.

You	**Buonasera. Ho una prenotazione.**
Signore	**Il suo nome, per favore?**
You	**Webb.**
Signore	**Ah sì. Il signor Webb. Una singola con doccia per tre notti.**
You	**Esatto.**
Signore	**Ha un documento, per piacere?**
You	**Sì. Il passaporto.**
Signore	**La camera è la trecentonove. Si trova al terzo piano. Questa è la chiave.**

45

You check the availability of rooms and you are lucky to be offered a double room with a private bathroom at a price you can afford.

You	**Buonasera. Ha una camera?**
Signora	**Per quanto tempo? Per questa notte?**
You	**Sì, per oggi e domani.**
Signora	**Sì, ho una doppia con bagno.**
You	**Quanto costa?**
Signora	**Sessantamila, tutto compreso.**
You	**Sì, va bene. La prendo.**

REPLAY

1 The size of your tent may be asked for as you check in. You can tell them: **è una grande/piccola tenda**. (It's a big/small tent.) A caravan is generally referred to as **una roulotte**.

2 You may well be asked these questions with **quanto**:
per quanto tempo? – How long are you staying?
per quante persone? – For how many people?

3 If you are planning on staying only one day, you can say: **solo per oggi** (only for today). Two days would be: **per oggi e domani** (today and tomorrow). **Una settimana** is a week.

4 If you want to see your room before deciding, you should ask: **posso vedere la camera?** If you decide to take it, say **la prendo**.

WORDQUIZ

1 *Don't get floored!:* Assume that the hotel's rooms are numbered logically with the first digit indicating the floor level. Match these keys to the floors they are on.

a   b   c

i **al primo piano**   ii **al secondo piano**
       iii **al terzo piano**

2 *Questions and answers:* Match a question from the right-hand column with its answer on the left.

a Per una settimana.   i Per quante persone?
b Cinquantamila.   ii Quanto costa?
c Due adulti.   iii Per quanto tempo?

3 *No napping:* Which of the following could you not really sleep in?   a **una singola**   b **una tenda**
       c **una doccia**   d **una doppia**

FACTSHEET 9: HOTELS AND CAMP-SITES

According to official records, Italy has over forty thousand hotels. These include **alberghi** in the five-star luxury category and simple, family-run guest houses known as **pensioni**. Clean and functional motels can also be found on some of the main motorways. If you see the sign **camere** it means there are vacancies, but if you see the sign **completo**, you are unlucky – the place is completely full. One little piece of information about the price. You pay usually for the room only. Even if the price is quoted as **tutto compreso**, the cost of breakfast will probably *not* be included. Breakfast, by the way, is **la prima colazione**.

Camp-sites, too, are plentiful, especially in the popular coastal areas (where it is particularly advisable to book in advance). It is also best to go armed with an International Camping Carnet, obtainable from your AA or RAC office. This entitles you to a small discount and provides minimum third-party insurance cover.

There are about fifty youth hostels (**ostelli della gioventù**). To find out where they are and how to go about booking, write to:
The Italian Youth Hostel Association (AIG),
Quadrato della Concordia, 9, 00144 Rome.

WORKOUT

1 You, your partner and your two small children arrive late one evening at a camp-site anxious to know whether there is any space left. What do you ask?

2 You are asked: **Per quante persone?** What is your reply?

3 You are staying only two nights, so how do you respond to this question? **Per questa notte?**

4 You arrive at a hotel having already phoned and booked from the **Azienda di Soggiorno e Turismo**. What do you tell the receptionist?

5 After you have given your name the receptionist says: **Ah sì, una doppia con bagno.** But you correct her by saying: 'No. A single with a shower'.

ON THE BEACH

WHEN IN ITALY ...

Italy, so the geographers tell us, has 5345 miles (8600 km) of coastline. A lot of beach space in the resorts is reserved for the guests of the nearby hotels. Other parts are also **spiaggia privata** (private beach), with charges for the use of facilities. Even in the most select resorts, however, there will be a stretch of sand or shingle which remains **spiaggia libera** (public beach), free for all to use.

• Saying what you would like:

Vorrei
un ombrellone.	(a sunshade)
una sdraia.	(a deckchair)
un pedalò.	(a pedal boat)
un lettino.	(a sunbed)

• Asking if you can hire something:

Posso noleggiare
un windsurf?	(a sailboard)
una bicicletta?	(a bicycle)

ACTION You can hear these conversations on cassette side B.

You equip yourself and your friend for a day on the beach,
with sunshade and deckchair. The beach attendant (**il
bagnino**) gives you the prices.

You	**Buongiorno.**
Bagnino	**Buongiorno.**
You	**Vorrei un ombrellone. Quanto costa?**
Bagnino	**Seimila lire tutto il giorno.**
You	**Seimila lire. E una sdraia?**
Bagnino	**Anche. Anche seimila, sì.**

You decide you'd like to have a go on the pedalo.

You	**Posso noleggiare un pedalo?**
Bagnino	**Certo signore.**
You	**Quanto costa?**
Bagnino	**Diecimila lire l'ora.**

You ask if it's OK to go swimming, and find out that the beach isn't private and the lake is clean.

You	**Posso fare il bagno qua?**
Bagnino	**Sì, le spiaggie non sono private. Il lago è pulito. Questo è molto importante.**

REPLAY
1 Vorrei (I would like) can be followed by the things you'd like or the things you'd like to do. For example, telephone home: **Vorrei telefonare in Inghilterra.**
2 The full name for a deckchair is **una sedia a sdraio.** Sometimes, however, you will hear it called **la sdraia, lo sdraio** or even **la sdraio.** So why should you worry too much about word endings!
3 Un'ora is 'an hour', whereas **l'ora** is 'the hour'. **Una mezz'ora** is 'half an hour'. **L'ora** also means 'time' in the question **ha l'ora?** (Have you got the time?)
4 Il bagno, as well as being the bathroom, means swimming. **Fare il bagno:** to go for a swim.

FACTSHEET 10: BESIDE THE SEA

Italian beaches, like those in other Mediterranean countries, can get very busy when everyone decides to soak up the sun. At the height of the summer the sun can be very hot indeed, so a shady spot under the **ombrellone** is a necessary protection from sunburn.

If you enjoy water sports, you will find that there is plenty to keep you occupied. Swimming (**il nuoto** or **il bagno**) is something most people enjoy, either in the pool (**in piscina**) or in the sea (**nel mare**). The proper Italian word for a sailboard is **una tavola a vela** (literally 'a table with a sail') but most people seem to end up using the international word **windsurf.** Sailing is just **la vela.** Fishing is **la pesca.** Curiously, that's the word for a peach, too!

WORDQUIZ

1 *Off the beach:* Which of the following items would you not expect to find on the beach:

a **un pedalò**   b **una sdraia**   c **un blocchetto**
d **una doccia**   e **un ombrellone**

2 *Higher prices:* Look back through the conversations. Can you work out how much the day cost you? (Don't forget the pedalo!)

3 *Letter fill:* The gaps in the following words are all consonants. Can you fill them in?

a o__e__o_e   b __ia__ia
c _o__ei   d _e__i_o

WORKOUT

1 You have just arrived at the beach. Tell the **bagnino** that you'd like a sunshade and a deckchair.
2 He tells you the price of the deckchair but forgets to mention the sunshade. Ask him how much that is.
3 You've had enough of the beach so you decide to try and hire a bicycle. How would you ask where it's possible to do that?
4 You think an hour's cycling will be enough. What phrase would you use?

a **per due ore**   b **solo per oggi**   c **solo per una mezz'ora**   d **un'ora solo**

5 You are touring along the coast and decide to stop for a dip. Just as you are about to step on the beach a woman calls to you. Can you work out what she is telling you?

Questa è privata. La spiaggia libera è a duecento metri a destra.

TRAVELLING BY CAR

WHEN IN ITALY …
If you are planning to take your car to Italy you'll be
pleased to know that foreign tourists can get 15%
discount off the price of petrol and motorway tolls. Petrol
coupons (**buoni di benzina**) and motorway toll vouchers
(**buoni pedaggio autostrade**) can be bought at the
frontier but, better still, in advance from AA or RAC
offices or from CIT (50 Conduit Street, London W1).
When the coupons run out, however, you will have to
resort to hard cash … and some simple Italian.
There are three ways of buying petrol:

• by far the easiest – by buying a full tank:
Il pieno, per favore.

• by stating the quantity required:
Trenta litri di super, per favore.

• by saying how much you want to spend:
Cinquantamila lire di super, per favore.

ACTION   You can hear the conversations on cassette side B.
You find that filling up at a country service station is a
very smooth operation.

Attendant	**Buonasera. Deve fare il pieno?**
You	**Sì, il pieno di super, per favore. Quant'è?**
Attendant	**Ventinovemila.**

You ask if you can pay with petrol coupons.

You	**Lei prende i buoni di benzina?**
Attendant	**I buoni? Sì, i coupons, sì.**
You	**Ah, benissimo.**

An Italian service station (**stazione di servizio**) may also
have a snack-bar attached, and other essential facilities.
You ask where the toilets are.

You	**Scusi, signora, dov'è la toilette?**
Signora	**E laggiù, dietro la cassa, in fondo a destra.**
You	**In fondo a destra.**

REPLAY

1 Pieno literally means 'full'. **Di** is used in many different expressions of quantity: **il pieno di super**; **il pieno di normale**; **trenta litri di super**; **cinquantamila lire di normale**.

2 To ask whether a garage takes coupons, look out for the sign COUPONS. Or ask the attendant **prende?** (do you take …?): **prende i buoni di benzina?** Use **prende?** also to check whether a garage, shop, hotel or restaurant accepts credit cards or traveller's cheques. Show your card or cheque and say: **prende questo?**

3 Petrol (**la benzina**) comes in two grades, **super** – equivalent to 4-star, and **normale** – 2-star quality. Diesel fuel (**il gasolio**) is much cheaper than petrol and available everywhere. Unleaded petrol is **senza piombo.**

4 Dietro means 'behind'; 'in front' is **davanti**.

FACTSHEET 11: CARWISE

Petrol

Italian service stations close for holidays on a rota basis, so don't be surprised to come across the sign **chiuso per turno**. On motorways, a 24-hour service is guaranteed.

Documents

As well as the usual papers, such as log-book and insurance certificate, you must take a translation of your driving licence (**la patente**). This can be obtained from the AA or RAC free of charge. There is no need to bother with this if you already have a pink EEC International driving licence. If you buy petrol coupons you will also be given a **carta carburante** (fuel card). This will entitle you to the free breakdown service provided by ACI (**Automobile Club d'Italia**). To contact ACI in an emergency, dial 116 at the nearest phone-box. Don't forget to carry an emergency warning triangle with you!

Motorway driving

Italy has a spectacular network of motorways stretching six thousand kilometres from the northern frontier points to the western coast of Sicily. Only the southernmost stretches are free; for the rest you have to pay a toll (**pedaggio**). To find your way to the motorway (**autostrada**), look for green signs with the appropriate number A1, A2 etc. To leave the motorway, look for the sign marked **uscita** (exit). Ordinary roads are SS (**Strade Statali**) and their signs have blue backgrounds.

WORDQUIZ

1 *Your number is up!:* These numbers are written back to front. Work out what they are, say them aloud a few times, and write down the number figures.

a **alimatnauqnic** b **alimevonitnev** c **alimottoicid**
d **alimorttauqatnert**

2 *Question words:* Match the words on the right with the words on the left to make sensible questions.

Dov'è	di super?
Prende	la toilette?
Il pieno	i buoni di benzina?

3 *Five times five:* Unscramble these five five-letter words.
a **cssui** b **ssaac** c **nofdo** d **iboun** e **ipoen**

WORKOUT

1 You are on the service station forecourt. Take part in this short conversation.

Attendant **Buongiorno. Le faccio il pieno?**
You (Say 'Yes. Fill it up with super, please.')
Attendant **Ecco. Quarantaduemilacinquecento.**
You (You didn't quite get that price. Say: 'I'm sorry, I don't understand.')

2 The attendant writes it down for you. What is the number he writes?

3 You need the toilet. What is the question you should ask?

4 You are told: **in fondo a sinistra**. Do you look on the right or the left?

5 As you leave the attendant wishes you a good journey. Does he say:

a **Buongiorno!** b **Buon viaggio!** c **Buoni di benzina!**

TAKING A TRIP

WHEN IN ITALY ...

If you want to organise your own excursions (**gite**) you should be able to get information and perhaps even book tickets at the local **Azienda di Turismo.** Otherwise go to the bus station (**autostazione**) or the railway station (**stazione ferroviaria**).

- Buying tickets is easy enough:

Due biglietti, per favore.

(Two tickets, please.)

Andata; andata e ritorno.

(single; return)

- Checking departure/arrival times:

A che ora parte/arriva?

(What time does it leave/arrive?)

- Finding somewhere to sit:

E libero questo posto?

(Is this place free?)

ACTION   You can hear these conversations on cassette side B.

You buy two return tickets for a trip to Naples.

You	**Buongiorno. Due biglietti per Napoli. Andata e ritorno.**

You want to get a coach from Rome to the village of Bracciano, so you ask at the bus station. You're told they leave every two hours.

You	**Scusi, c'è un pullman per Bracciano?**
Inspector	**Sì.**
You	**A che ora parte?**
Inspector	**Ogni due ore. Lì, c'è l'orario.**

You ask when the plane arrives in Rome.

You	**Quando si arriva a Roma?**
Steward	**Si arriva tra cinquanta minuti – alle dieci.**

On a crowded train you ask if a seat is free.

You   **Scusi, è libero questo posto?**
Passenger **Sì, prego.**

REPLAY

1 Just one ticket is **un biglietto**. You can just say:
uno per ... plus your destination. If you're travelling
with young children, you can ask for a reduced fare (**un
ridotto**).
2 On a timetable (**orario**), the key words are: **arrivi**
(arrivals), **partenze** (departures), and **coincidenze**
(connecting services).
3 To get a general idea of when you will arrive at your
destination, you can ask: **Quando si arriva a . . . ?**
(When do we arrive at . . . ?) **Tra cinquanta minuti** is 'in
fifty minutes' time'.
4 Libero means free in the sense both of 'empty' and 'no
charge'. If a seat is taken, or a toilet cubicle occupied, the
word used is **occupato**.
5 Prego, as well as being a polite reply to someone
saying 'thank you', can be a signal for you to go ahead or
to carry on what you were doing.

WORDQUIZ

1 *Just the ticket:* Sort out these jumbled words and you
should get the names of three different tickets.

a **tadana**   b **dirtoto**   c **reattinoordana**

2 Choose one of these words to fill the gap

a **occupato**   b **ore**   c **pullman**   d **orario**

Il treno per Terni parte ogni due ....

FACTSHEET 12: TRAVELLING ABROAD

Tickets

These can be bought in a proper ticket office (**una biglietteria**). There is usually one of these in or near the railway station or the bus station. Children under twelve travel half fare on Italian trains. If you are planning to travel extensively by train, there's just the ticket for you. It's called **un biglietto turistico libera circolazione**. This entitles you to unlimited mileage over 8, 15, 21 or 30 days depending on the price you pay.

Trains

There are several types of train in Italy, and ticket prices vary accordingly. **Un diretto** may sound fast and direct, but isn't really. In a hurry, better take **un espresso**, or better still **un rapido**. The TEE (Trans Europe Express) is the quickest way to get from A to Z, but with first class travel only *and* a surcharge on ticket prices, it is very expensive. To find the right platform you should ask: **Che binario per ...?** naming your destination.

Timetables

As you study the arrival and departure times make sure you distinguish between weekdays, which are **giorni feriali,** and Sundays and public holidays, called **giorni festivi**.

WORKOUT

1 At the tourist office you hear details of a trip to the island of Capri. Ask what time the ferry leaves. A ferry is **un traghetto**.

2 You want a return ticket. How do you reply when you are asked by the ticket salesman: **Andata o andata e ritorno?**

3 You want to know when the coach gets into Florence. Ask the driver.

4 You're taking a train trip to Pisa. Ask which platform you should head for.

BEING SOCIABLE

WHEN IN ITALY ...
Here are some more conversational gambits to go with
the phrases from 'Making Contact' (Progetto 3).

● Asking 'how are you?'
Come sta?

● Introducing someone:
Questo è il mio amico/mio marito.
(This is my friend/husband.)
Questa è la mia amica/mia moglie.
(This is my friend/wife.)

● Talking about children:
Ha figli?   (Do you have any children?)
Quanti anni ha?   (How old is he/she?)

● Asking about someone's job:
Che lavoro fa?

ACTION   You can hear these conversations on cassette side B.
You bump into Elena again, and she asks how you are.

You	**Buongiorno.**
Elena	**Come sta?**
You	**Benissimo grazie, e lei?**
Elena	**Non c'è male.**

She introduces a friend.

Elena	**Questo è il mio amico Fabrizio.**
You	**Piacere.**
Fabrizio	**Come sta?**

She asks you about your family.

Elena	**Ha figli?**
You	**Sì, mia figlia ha tre anni e mio figlio ha cinque anni.**

61

You ask her about work.

You	**Che lavoro fa?**
Elena	**Lavoro in una pizzeria, e lei?**
You	**Io insegno.**

REPLAY

1 To ask how someone is feeling, say **come sta?** when addressing an adult whom you don't know very well. Later you can switch to the more familiar **come stai?** Answers will range from **sto bene**, or just **bene** (I'm fine) to **benissimo, grazie** (very well, thanks). **Non c'è male** can be summed up as 'not too bad'.

2 A neat phrase to use when being introduced to someone: **piacere** (it's a pleasure), accompanied by a handshake.

3 To say what work you do, either say where you work (**lavoro in . . .**) or use **sono** + the occupation, e.g. **sono infermiera** (I am a nurse). Or simply say what you do e.g. **io insegno** (I teach).

4 To describe your family, start with **ho** (I have) followed by the number of daughters (**figlie**) and sons (**figli**). If you have no children, say **non ho figli**.

WORDQUIZ

1 *Short cuts:* Separate these 'words' where necessary to create sensible sentences.

a **questoèmiomaritoluigi**   b **chelavorofa?**
c **miofigliohadodicianniemiafigliahanoveanni**

2 *My! My!:* Match the correct form of 'my' with the person on the right.

mia	marito
il mio	figlia
mio	amico
mia	moglie

FACTSHEET 13: ITALIAN FAMILIES

Italians adore children. If you go to Italy with babies or toddlers don't be surprised or shocked to have them whisked away amid cries of **Oh che bel bambino!** if it's a boy, or **Che bella bambina!** if it's a girl. Don't worry, you will get your offspring back eventually.

It is true that the Italian family is quite an institution – but things are changing. Despite their adoration of babies, fewer Italians are opting for the roles of **mamma** and **papà**. The birth rate in Italy is declining dramatically and large families are a thing of the past, especially in the expensive, industrial north. Statistics from Genoa tell us that in the city and surrounding region about 30 people die each day but only 10 new **Genovesi** come into the world to take their place.

WORKOUT

1 A new Italian acquaintance has just introduced you to her husband. Which of these phrases would be quite inappropriate?

a **Come sta?**   b **Mi piace.**   c **Piacere.**

2 You are asked how you are feeling. Say: 'Not too bad, thanks'.

3 The conversation turns to families. You are asked if you have children. What's the question?

4 You want to find out about his job – what question should you ask?

DEALING WITH DIFFICULTIES

WHEN IN ITALY ....
Everybody hopes for a trouble-free holiday, but in case
something gets broken or lost here are some useful
phrases.

- Reporting that something is broken:

E guasto.

- Getting something repaired:

Può riparare questo?

- Saying you have left/lost something somewhere:

Ho lasciato/ho perso ...

64

ACTION You can hear these conversations on cassette side B.

You report a broken telephone to the hotel receptionist.

You	**Il telefono è guasto.**
Receptionist	**Che numero è la sua camera?**
You	**Trecentonove.**
Receptionist	**Va bene. Ci vado subito.**

Your glasses need mending, so you go into a **foto-ottica** to see if they can help.

Shopkeeper	**Mi dica.**
You	**Può riparare questo?**
Shopkeeper	**Vediamo un po'. Sì, non c'è problema. Torni fra dieci minuti.**
You	**Fra dieci minuti. Grazie.**

You think you left your wallet in a shop, so you go back.

You	**Scusi, ho lasciato il portafoglio?**
Assistant	**Di che colore è?**
You	**E bianco e nero.**
Assistant	**E questo il suo?**
You	**Ah, sì, è il mio. Mille grazie.**

REPLAY

1 The last letter of **guasto** (broken or broken down) will vary according to the thing mentioned. See page 74 for help with these changes of word ending. Other things that might go wrong are **la macchina** (car); **la doccia** (shower); **l'ascensore** (lift); **la serratura** (lock).

2 To ask about colours the question starts with: **di che colore è …?** Italians say 'white and black' (**bianco e nero**) whereas we say 'black and white'.

3 The polite way to say 'your' is **il suo** or **la sua**: **il suo portafoglio** (your wallet); **la sua valigia** (your suitcase). 'My' or 'mine' is **il mio** or **la mia**. With close members of the family you don't need **il** or **la** – e.g. **mio marito**.

4 For really heartfelt thanks you can add **mille** (a thousand) to **grazie** (thanks).

5 **Torni fra dieci minuti** means 'come back in ten minutes'.

WORDQUIZ

1 *Broken bits:* Several things are wrong here, including the spelling. Can you work out what needs repairing? (Tip: Note 1 above may help here.)

a **La ratursear è guasta.** c **La cadioc è guasta.**
b **Il feeltoon è guasto.**   d **La nahacimc è guasta.**

2 *Gap fill:* Choose a word from the list provided to complete these questions. Careful! There are more words than gaps.

a **C'è _____ problema?**
b **Il suo _____ per favore?**
c **Che numero è la _____ camera?**
d **Di che _____ è?**
e **_____ riparare questo?**

una – sua – bene – può – colore – nome – mio – un

FACTSHEET 14: GETTING HELP

Medical matters

For minor ailments and non-prescription medicines advice will be freely given at the chemist's (**la farmacia**). If you need the doctor (**il medico**) it is here that you will find a list of those on duty, day and night. You should take along to the surgery your Form E111, obtainable from your local Social Security Office. For more urgent medical assistance, the casualty department (**il pronto soccorso**) of the nearest hospital (**l'ospedale**) will be the best place to go. It hurts is **fa male**.

Phoning home

Instead of fussing around with telephone tokens (**gettoni**) or lots of coins (**moneta**) you can do two things to speed up the operation. You can buy a telephone card (**una carta telefonica**) and use one of the special telephone booths. Or you can use a telephone in a hotel, or in a bar where you can see the yellow sign with a telephone receiver on it. Here, your call is timed in units (**scatti**) and you pay afterwards according to the number you have used. When dialling Britain, remember to omit the '0' from the area code.

To dial the emergency services throughout Italy, the number is 113.

WORKOUT

1 You check into a hotel and as you leave the reception desk the porter calls out to you: **Signore, mi dispiace, l'ascensore è guasto.** What is he telling you?

2 You can't find the hotel key, but you discover a hole in your pocket. How do you report the loss to the receptionist?

3 You've got a flat tyre (**una gomma** is a tyre) and you ask the garage man if he can repair it.

4 You are told to come back **fra trenta minuti.** How long have you got for a coffee?

EATING OUT

WHEN IN ITALY …
Eating in **un ristorante** tends to be more expensive than in **una trattoria,** while the cheapest place for a meal is usually **una pizzeria** or **una tavola calda**.

- To ask for the menu:
Il menu, per favore.

- To order a first course (**primo**) or a main course (**secondo**), just name the dish.
spaghetti al pomodoro (spaghetti with tomato sauce)
bistecca (steak)

- Ordering drinks with the meal:
una bottiglia di vino bianco (bottle of white wine)
un'acqua minerale (mineral water)

- Asking for the bill:
Il conto, per favore.

ACTION You can hear these conversations on cassette side B.

You are eating out with a friend. You order two pasta dishes to start the meal.

Waiter	**Buonasera, signori. Per primo, cosa prendono?**
You	**Spaghetti alle vongole e tagliatelle al ragù, per favore.**
Waiter	**Molto bene.**

You then order drinks: a bottle of the local white wine and some mineral water.

Waiter	**E da bere?**
You	**Una bottiglia di vino bianco.**
Waiter	**Il vino locale. Va bene?**
You	**Sì. E un'acqua minerale gassata, per favore.**
Waiter	**Va bene.**
You	**E un po' di pane, per favore.**

The waiter checks that you are happy with your meal so far and takes the order for the main course – steak in a garlic and tomato sauce for you, and veal cutlet for your friend, accompanied by mixed salad and chips.

Waiter	**Tutto bene?**
You	**Sì, grazie. È molto buono.**
Waiter	**Per secondo, signori, cosa prendono?**
You	**Una bistecca alla pizzaiola per me . . .**
	. . . e una cotoletta alla milanese per il mio amico.
Waiter	**E come contorno?**
You	**Un'insalata mista e patate fritte.**

After your dessert, you signal to the waiter to bring the bill.

You	**Senta, il conto per favore.**
Waiter	**Subito, signora.**

REPLAY

1 Cosa prendono? cosa desiderano? and **cosa preferiscono?** are all ways you might be asked what you're having. **E da bere?** is the invitation to order the drinks.

2 Mineral water comes in two varieties, **gassata** (fizzy) and **naturale** (still). If you don't need a whole bottle, ask for **una mezza minerale** (half a litre).

WORDQUIZ

1 *Missing consonants:* Make four words to do with eating out by filling in the gaps with suitable consonants.

a _o_o_e__a b _i__e_ia
c _o__i__ia d __a__e__i

2 *Twisted pasta:* Untwist the following words to make three pasta dishes.

a **atesghipt** b **elaltilegta** c **viliroa**

3 *Meal break:* Match a word from the left-hand column with the most suitable one from the right-hand side.

a insalata	i fritte
b vino	ii mista
c patate	iii bianco
d acqua	iv minerale

WORKOUT

1 You and your friend are dining out, and you are doing all the talking. Ask the waiter what the local wine is called.

2 Tell him you will also have a bottle of mineral water, of the non-fizzy variety.

3 The waiter asks: **Come contorno?** Order mixed salad for yourself and tomato salad for your companion. (Say: 'a salad of tomatoes'.)

4 At the end of your meal you decide to have two coffees. Ask for the bill at the same time.

5 *Menu mix up:* Match the order with the right question. Then list them in the order they are likely to occur in a restaurant.

a E da bere?	i Patate fritte.
b E come contorno?	ii Sì, un espresso.
c Per primo?	iii Un'acqua minerale.
d Prende un caffè?	iv Bistecca.
e E come secondo?	v Ravioli, per favore.

FACTSHEET 15: ORDERING MEALS

A full meal in Italy will consist of **un antipasto** (a starter such as ham or melon), **un primo** (usually one from a selection of pasta dishes), **un secondo** (the main meat or fish dish), and fruit, cheese or **un dolce** (a sweet item such as cake). Generally, people have a pasta and a main course or antipasto and a main course.

The vegetables or salads accompanying the main course are referred to as **contorni**, and they come separately. The waiter will ask: **Come contorno?** (What will you have as a vegetable?) People take only one usually. Most common among the **contorni** on a typical **menu turistico** are **insalata mista** (mixed salad) and **patate fritte** (chips). If you want to know about vegetarian dishes ask **C'è un piatto vegetariano?**

If there is no menu to hand, the people serving you may rattle off a long list of the dishes available. To slow them down just say: **Lentamente, per favore!** The cover charge, which should be stated on the menu, includes the cost of bread. Look for the price next to the item **pane e coperto**. The service (**servizio**) varies between 10% – 15% and is generally added to the bill.
To help you understand menus there's a word list on pages 82-3.

A VERY BASIC GRAMMAR

CONTENTS

1 'A' and 'THE'
Italian naming words (nouns) are either masculine (m) or feminine (f) and the word for 'a' or 'the' changes accordingly.

Feminine words
Many feminine words end in 'a', e.g. **strada** (street), **birra** (beer). In this case the words for 'a' and 'the' also end in 'a'.

una strada a street   **la strada** the street
una birra a beer   **la birra** the beer

If the noun begins with a vowel (a,e,i,o,u) 'a' is **un'** and 'the' is **l'**.

un'amica a girl friend   **l'amica** the girl friend

With feminine words in the plural, the word for 'the' is **le**, and quite often the last letter of the noun will also be 'e'.
le birre the beers   **le amiche** the girl friends

Masculine words
Many masculine words end in 'o', e.g. **treno** (train), **posto** (place). For most masculine words, the word for 'a' is **un** and 'the' is **il**.

un treno a train   **il treno** the train
un posto a place   **il posto** the place

If a masculine noun begins with a vowel, you still use **un** but the word for 'the' is **l'**.

un amico a boy friend   **l'amico** the boy friend

If a masculine word begins with a 'z' or 's' followed by another consonant (b,c,d,f,g,l, etc.) the word for 'a' is **uno** and the word for 'the' is **lo**.

uno zucchero   a lump of sugar
lo zucchero   the sugar
uno scontrino   a receipt
lo scontrino   the receipt

With masculine words in the plural, the word for 'the' will be either **i** (for most nouns) or **gli** (for those starting with 'z' or 's' plus a consonant). The last letter of the noun will also end in 'i' in most cases.

i treni the trains
i posti the places
gli scontrini the receipts

Words ending in 'e'

Quite a number of words end in 'e'. They may be either masculine or feminine.

il mare (m)   the sea | **la patente** (f) the driving licence

In the plural these words will end in 'i'.

i mari   the seas | **le patenti** the driving licences

2 AGREEMENTS

Words that describe things or people, such as 'beautiful' or 'big' or 'ripe', are called adjectives. In Italian they usually come after the words they describe. Their endings change, depending on the word they are with. Look for the patterns of endings in these examples.

una pesca matura   a ripe peach
due pesche mature   two ripe peaches
un pomodoro maturo   a ripe tomato
due pomodori maturi   two ripe tomatoes

Adjectives ending in 'e' only change with words in the plural.

la mela verde   the green apple
le mele verdi   the green apples
il formaggio dolce   the mild cheese
i formaggi dolci   the mild cheeses

3 'I', 'YOU' and OTHER PEOPLE

In Italian you don't need to use the words for 'I', 'you', 'he', 'she', 'it', etc. as much as you do in English, because the verb endings (see 4 below) show who is talking or being referred to.

'I' is **io**
'you' is **tu** (to a child or friend)
'you' is **lei** (for polite, more formal use with one person)
'you' is **voi** (talking to more than one person)
'he' or 'him' is **lui**
'she' or 'her' is **lei**
'we' or 'us' is **noi**
'they' or 'them' is **loro**

4 VERBS

Verbs are words describing actions. In any language verbs tend to be the most complicated bits of sentences. Italian is no exception! But to help you cope in simple situations, here is a summary of what you should be able to say after reading *When in Italy*.

basta così – that's enough
capisco – I understand
c'è – there is
è – it is, you (**lei**) are
ho – I have
(N.B. **ho venti anni** – I am 20)
ho lasciato – I have left
ho perso – I have lost
mi chiamo . . . – my name is
mi dà – give me
mi dispiace – I am sorry
mi piace – I like
parlo – I speak
posso – I can
preferisco – I prefer
prendo – I'll take
scusi – excuse me
sono – I am
sto – I feel, I am staying
va bene (così) – that's OK
vorrei – I would like

Non in front of a verb makes it negative.

e.g. **non capisco** – I don't understand,
non mi piace – I don't like

5 QUESTIONS

Questions are easier in Italian than in English! Convert statements into questions by saying them with an inquiring tone. Listen to the end of Side B on the cassette.

Posso?	Can I?
Parla inglese?	Do you speak English?
C'è una banca qui vicino?	Is there a bank near here?

These are the essential question words of *When in Italy:*

Che?	What?
Che numero?	What number or size?
Che taglia?	What size?
A che ora?	At what time
Di che colore?	What colour?
Come?	What? or How?
Come si chiama?	What's your name?
Come sta?	How are you feeling?
Cosa?	What?
Cosa prende?	What will you have? (to eat or drink)
Dove?	Where?
Dov'è?	Where is?
Dove sono?	Where are?
Quale?	Which?
Quale preferisce?	Which do you prefer?
Quando?	When?
Quanto?	How much? How many?
Quant'è?	How much does it come to?
Quante persone?	How many people?
Quanti anni ha?	How old is he/she?
Quanti anni hanno?	How old are they?

USEFUL WORDS

In this section you'll find three lists giving words you might need in the following situations:
1 When shopping
2 Emergencies and difficulties
3 When travelling

There's also a menu-guide (4), a list of numbers (5), and a list of dates (6).

1 WHEN SHOPPING

Shops and services

baker's	**una panetteria; un panificio**
bank	**una banca**
butcher's	**una macelleria**
camera shop	**una foto-ottica**
chemist's	**una farmacia**
dry cleaners	**un lavasecco**
greengrocer's	**un fruttivendolo**
grocer's	**un alimentari**
post office	**la posta**
post-box	**una cassetta (delle lettere)**
shoe shop	**una calzoleria**
supermarket	**un supermercato**
tourist office	**un ufficio di turismo**
telephone exchange	**la SIP**

Groceries

bag	**una borsa;** plastic bag **una bustina**
biscuits	**i biscotti**
bread	**il pane**
bread rolls	**i panini**
butter	**il burro**
cheese	**il formaggio**
coffee	**il caffè**
egg(s)	**un'uovo** (plural: **uova**)
ham	**il prosciutto**
margarine	**la margarina**

oil	l'olio
olive	un'oliva
pasta	la pasta
rice	il riso
tea	il tè
vinegar	l'aceto
yoghurt	lo yogurt
tin of . . .	una lattina di. . .
bottle of . . .	una bottiglia di. . .

Drinks

beer	la birra
fruit juice	il succo di frutta
lemonade	la gassosa
milk (fresh/skimmed)	il latte (fresco/scremato)
mineral water (fizzy)	l'acqua minerale (gassata)
wine	il vino

Fruit and veg

apple	una mela
banana	una banana
bean (green)	un fagiolo (fagiolino)
fig	un fico
garlic	l'aglio
grapefruit	un pompelmo
lemon	un limone
lettuce	un'insalata
melon	un melone
nectarine	una nocepesca
onion	una cipolla
orange	un'arancia
pear	una pera
potato	una patata
tomato	un pomodoro
water-melon	un cocomero

Clothes

dress	un vestito
hat	un cappello
jacket	una giacca
knitwear	una maglia
pants	uno slip
shirt or blouse	una camicia

shoes	le scarpe
skirt	una gonna
socks	le calze
suit	un abito
sunglasses	gli occhiali da sole
swimming costume	il costume da bagno
tights	il collant
trousers	i pantaloni

Others

film	la pellicola
nappies	i pannolini
soap	il sapone
suntan cream	la crema abbronzante
tampons	i tamponi assorbenti
tissues	i fazzoletti
toilet paper	la carta igienica
toothpaste	il dentifricio
towel	un asciugamano

2 EMERGENCIES AND DIFFICULTIES

Phrases

Look out!	Attenzione!
Stop!	Fermi! Stop!
Leave me alone!	Mi lasci in pace!
Help!	Aiuto!
Quick!	Presto!
Call the police	Chiami la polizia.
Call a doctor.	Chiami un medico.
I'm ill.	Sono malato/a.
I've lost. . .	Ho perso. . .

Things you might lose or leave behind

camera	la macchina fotografica
contact lenses	le lenti a contatto
credit card	la carta di credito
glasses	gli occhiali
handbag	la borsetta
key	la chiave
money	i soldi
passport	il passaporto
suitcase	la valigia

3 WHEN TRAVELLING

By car

battery	**la batteria**
broken down	**guasto/a**
car	**la macchina**
caravan	**la roulotte**
car-park	**il parcheggio**
to check	**controllare**
coupon	**il buono;** petrol coupons **i buoni di benzina;** motorway toll coupons **i buoni pedaggio autostrada**
diesel	**il gasolio**
driving licence	**la patente**
card	**la carta;** fuel token card **la carta carburante**
engine	**il motore**
exit	**l'uscita**
full	**pieno**
litre	**un litro**
motorbike	**la motocicletta**
motorway	**l'autostrada**
oil	**l'olio**
petrol	**la benzina**
	2 Star **il normale**
	4 Star **il super**
repair	**riparare**
service station	**la stazione di servizio**
street	**la strada**
toll	**il pedaggio**
tow	**il rimorchio**
traffic lights	**il semaforo**
tyre	**la gomma**
wheel	**la ruota**

By other means of transport

airport	**l'aeroporto**
Arrivals	**Arrivi**
book of tickets	**un blocchetto**
bus	**l'autobus**
bus station	**l'autostazione**

bus stop	**la fermata**
cable car	**la funivia**
coach	**il pullman**
connecting services	**le coincidenze**
Departures	**Partenze**
ferry	**il traghetto**
hydrofoil	**un aliscafo**
journey	**il viaggio;** have a good journey! **buon viaggio!**
late	**in ritardo**
to leave	**partire**
platform	**il binario**
railway station	**la stazione ferroviaria**
reduced fare	**il ridotto**
return	**un andata e ritorno**
single	**un andata**
strike	**uno sciopero**
ticket	**il biglietto**
timetable	**l'orario**
ticket office	**la biglietteria**
train	**il treno**

Sightseeing and holidaying

beach	**la spiaggia**
bicycle	**la bicicletta**
boat	**il battello;** small boat **la barca**
castle	**il castello**
cathedral	**il duomo**
church	**la chiesa**
deckchair	**la sdraia**
exhibition	**la mostra**
fountain	**la fontana**
guide	**la guida**
harbour	**il porto**
hire	**noleggiare**
island	**l'isola**
lake	**il lago**
mountain	**la montagna**
museum	**il museo**
sea (rough)	**il mare (mosso)**

shade	**l'ombra**
sun	**il sole**
sunbed	**il lettino**
sunshade	**l'ombrellone**
to swim	**fare il bagno**
swimming pool	**la piscina**
weather	**il tempo;** it's nice/not nice **fa bel/brutto tempo**

4 MENU-GUIDE

Starters (antipasti)

antipasto di mare seafood salad
antipasto misto selection of salamis and cold meats
bresaola dried salted beef
crostini toasted bread with cheese, chopped liver or other toppings
prosciutto e melone ham with melon
tonno e fagioli tuna and beans

Soups (zuppe)

brodo broth
minestrone thick vegetable soup
stracciatella clear soup with egg
zuppa di pesce fish soup

Fish (pesci)

acciughe anchovies
anguilla eel
aragosta lobster
calamari squid
frutti del mare or **fritto misto** mixed sea-food
luccio pike
sogliola sole
trota trout

Meat (carni)

agnello lamb
coniglio rabbit
fegato liver
maiale pork
manzo beef
pollo arrosto roast chicken
spezzatino stew
vitello veal

Vegetables (contorni)

carciofi artichokes
cavolfiore cauliflower
cavolo cabbage
fagioli kidney beans
lesso boiled
melanzane aubergines
piselli peas
radicchio chicory
riso rice
sedano celery
zucchini courgettes

Cheeses (formaggi)

dolce latte mild blue
fontina fatty, semi-soft
gorgonzola soft, blue and yellow
groviera Gruyère
mozzarella soft and white, made with buffalo milk
parmigiano Parmesan, also known as **grana**
pecorino ewe's milk cheese
ricotta buttermilk cream cheese
stracchino white, slightly sour

Sweets (dolci)

affogato di caffè cake soaked in coffee
cassata ice-cream cake
frutta di stagione fruit in season
macedonia di frutta fruit salad
panna montata whipped cream
torta di casa home-made pie
zuppa inglese a rich kind of trifle without the fruit!

5 NUMBERS (I NUMERI)

1 uno	11 undici	21 ventuno
2 due	12 dodici	22 ventidue
3 tre	13 tredici	23 ventitré etc
4 quattro	14 quattordici	30 trenta
5 cinque	15 quindici	40 quaranta
6 sei	16 sedici	50 cinquanta
7 sette	17 diciassette	60 sessanta
8 otto	18 diciotto	70 settanta
9 nove	19 diciannove	80 ottanta
10 dieci	20 venti	90 novanta

100	cento	1000 mille
101	centuno	1500 millecinquecento
150	centocinquanta	5000 cinquemila
500	cinquecento	1 000 000 un milione
1989	millenovecentottantanove	

1st primo		6th sesto
2nd secondo		7th settimo
3rd terzo		8th ottavo
4th quarto		9th nono
5th quinto		10th decimo

6 DATES (LE DATE)

The days of the week (i giorni della settimana)

Monday	lunedì	Friday	venerdì
Tuesday	martedì	Saturday	sabato
Wednesday	mercoledì	Sunday	domenica
Thursday	giovedì	On Sundays	la domenica

The months of the year (i mesi dell'anno)

January	gennaio	July	luglio
February	febbraio	August	agosto
March	marzo	September	settembre
April	aprile	October	ottobre
May	maggio	November	novembre
June	giugno	December	dicembre

ANSWERS

PROGETTO 1

Wordquiz

1 *Unscramble*   a caffelatte   b aranciata   c cioccolata
2 *Doubling up*   a due tè e due cappuccini
b due birre e sei granite
c quattro caffè e due aranciate
3 *Attention please*
c scusi

Workout

1 No. Un tè al latte, per favore.
2 Due caffè, per favore.
3 Una birra, due aranciate e quattro granite al limone,
per favore.
4 b alla spina

PROGETTO 2

Wordquiz

1 *Watch your p's*   a pizza   b prego   c piazza   d pianta
2 *Odd one out*   b dépliant
3 *Open and shut*   b aperto

Workout

1 Scusi, c'è un ufficio turismo qui?
2 Ha una pianta della città?
3 Un listino campeggi, per favore.
4 C'è una banca qui?
5 No, grazie. Arrivederci.

PROGETTO 3

Wordquiz

1 *Roots*   a inglese   b scozzese   c irlandese
2 *City links*
GENOVA   MILANO   NAPOLI   TORINO   FIRENZE

Workout

1 Come si chiama?
2 Lei è di qui?
3 No, non sono di Londra. Sono gallese.
4 Mi chiamo. . .

PROGETTO 4

Wordquiz

1 *Front to back*	a Sì, un po'.
	b No, mi dispiace.
	c No. Non parlo molto italiano.
2 *Coping with stress*	b Parla italiano?
	c Scusi, non capisco.
	d Parlo soltanto italiano.
	e Come si chiama questo?
3 *I speak, you speak*	parla parli parlo
	(*Parlo* means 'I speak'.)

Workout

1 b non capisco
2 Parlo francese un po'. Non parlo molto italiano.
3 Come si chiama questo posto?
4 Do you speak German?

PROGETTO 5

Wordquiz

1 *Number sequences*

a tre	tredici	trentatré
b cinque	quindici	cinquantacinque
c otto	diciotto	ottantotto

2 *Pointing the way*   a ↰   b ↑   c ↱

3 *Near and far*

a lontano   b vicino   c lontano

Workout

1 Un blocchetto, per favore.
2 Che numero per via Magenta?
3 After two, i.e. the third stop.
4 Dov'è via Magenta, per favore?

PROGETTO 6

Wordquiz

1 *Number match*
  a millecinque – 1500
  b tremilaquattrocento – 3400
  c seimilasettecentocinquanta – 6750
  d quattromila – 4000

2 *Mixed flavours*
a caffè b limone c nocciola d fragola

Workout

1 Due panini, per favore.
Formaggio.
Quanto costa?
Ecco quattromila.

2 Un po' di questo, per favore.

3 Come si chiama in italiano?

PROGETTO 7

Wordquiz

1 *Weight-watching*

a ½kg	ii mezzo chilo
b 200g	iii due etti
c 1kg	iv un chilo
d 100g	i un etto

2 *Anything else?*
  a vuole altro?
  b e poi?
  c nient'altro?
  d basta così?

Workout

1 un chilo di pesche, due etti di formaggio, dieci panini, cinque fette di prosciutto, mezzo chilo di pomodori, e cinque mele.
2 Un po' di più, per favore.
3 No, basta così, grazie.
4 Quanto costa?
5 Duecentocinquanta (250) lire.

PROGETTO 8

Wordquiz

1 *Do your sums*
    a 1500 lire – millecinquecento
    b 2000 lire – duemila
    c 4000 lire – quattromila
    d 5000 lire – cinquemila

2 *Missing vowels*
    a E bellissimo, ma troppo caro.
    b Posso provare questo?
    c Ha francobolli per cartoline?

3 *Boxed in*

Mi dispiace, non parlo italiano.
a Starting top right, read each line backwards.
b Starting bottom right, read each line backwards.
c Starting bottom left, work up and then down.

Workout

1 Ha francobolli?
2 Più piccolo, per favore.
3 Posso provare questo?
4 Quanto costa?
5 b è molto bello
  d mi piace

PROGETTO 9

Wordquiz

1 *Don't get floored!*
    313 – al terzo piano
    122 – al primo piano
    250 – al secondo piano

2 *Questions and answers*
  i Per quante persone?   c Due adulti.
  ii Quanto costa?   b Cinquantamila.
  iii Per quanto tempo?   a Per una settimana.

3 *No napping*   c una doccia

Workout

1 Buonasera. C'è posto?
2 Per due adulti e due bambini.
3 Sì, per oggi e domani.
4 Ho una prenotazione.
5 No. Una singola con doccia.

PROGETTO 10

Wordquiz

1 *Off the beach*   c un blocchetto

2 *Higher prices*   22 000 lire

3 *Letter fill*
a ombrellone   b spiaggia   c vorrei   d lettino

Workout

1 Vorrei un ombrellone e una sdraia, per favore.
2 Quant'è l'ombrellone?
3 Dove posso noleggiare una bicicletta?
4 d un'ora solo
5 This is private. The public beach is two hundred metres on the right.

PROGETTO 11

Wordquiz

1 *Your number is up!*

a cinquantamila (50 000)   b ventinovemila (29 000)
c diciottomila (18 000)   d trentaquattromila (34 000)

2 *Question words* Dov'è la toilette?
                    Prende i buoni di benzina?
                    Il pieno di super?

3 *Five times five*
a scusi b cassa c fondo d buoni e pieno

Workout

1 Sì, il pieno di super, per favore.
Mi dispiace, non capisco.
2 42 500
3 Scusi, dov'è la toilette?
4 left
5 b Buon viaggio!

PROGETTO 12

Wordquiz

1 *Just the ticket*
a andata b ridotto   c andata e ritorno

2 b ore

Workout

1 A che ora parte il traghetto?
2 Andata e ritorno.
3 Quando si arriva a Firenze?
4 Che binario per Pisa?

PROGETTO 13

Wordquiz

1 *Short cuts*
a Questo è mio marito Luigi.
b Che lavoro fa?
c Mio figlio ha dodici anni e mia figlia ha nove anni.

2 *My! My!* mia figlia
il mio amico
mio marito
mia moglie

Workout

1 b Mi piace.
2 Non c'è male, grazie.
3 Ha figli?
4 Che lavoro fa?

PROGETTO 14

Wordquiz

1 *Broken bits*
a La serratura è guasta. c La doccia è guasta.
b Il telefono è guasto.   d La macchina è guasta.

2 *Gap fill* a C'è un problema?
b Il suo nome per favore?
c Che numero è la sua camera?
d Di che colore è?
e Può riparare questo?

Workout

1 The lift is broken.
2 Ho perso la mia chiave.
3 Può riparare la gomma?
4 30 minutes.

PROGETTO 15

Wordquiz

1 *Missing consonants*

a cotoletta b pizzeria c bottiglia d spaghetti

2 *Twisted pasta* a spaghetti b tagliatelle c ravioli

3 *Meal break* a insalata   ii   mista
                b vino   iii bianco
                c patate   i   fritte
                d acqua   iv   minerale

Workout

1 Come si chiama il vino locale?
2 E una bottiglia d'acqua minerale naturale.
3 Un'insalata mista e un'insalata di pomodori.
4 Due caffè e il conto, per favore.
5 *Menu mix up*

a Per primo?   v   Ravioli, per favore.
b E da bere?   iii Un'acqua minerale.
c E come secondo?   iv Bistecca.
d E come contorno?   i Patate fritte.
e Prende un caffè?   ii Sì, un espresso.

ITALIAN-ENGLISH VOCABULARY

a, al, alla, all' to the
l' **acqua** (f) water
l' **albergo** (m) hotel
alimentari general
stores
allora then
altro other, else
l' **amico/a** friend
anche also, too
andata single (ticket)
andata e ritorno return
(ticket)
l' **antipasto** (m) hors
d'oeuvre
aperto/a open
l' **arancia** (f) orange
l' **aranciata** (f) orangeade
arriva he or she
arrives
l' **autostrada** (f) motorway

il **bagnino** beach
attendant
il **bagno** bath, bathroom;
fare il bagno to go
swimming
il **bambino** baby boy
la **bambina** baby girl
basta that's enough
bellissimo/a very
beautiful
bello/a beautiful, fine
bene well, good
benissimo/a very well;
very good
la **benzina** petrol
bere to drink
bianco/a white
la **biglietteria** ticket office
il **biglietto** ticket
il **binario** platform
la **birra** beer
bisogna it is necessary
la **bistecca** steak

il **blocchetto** book of
tickets
la **borsa** bag
la **bottiglia** bottle
la **brioche** breakfast bun
buono/a good
buon appetito! have a
good meal!
buona vacanza! have a
good holiday!
buon viaggio! have a
good journey!
il **buono** coupon; **buono
di benzina** petrol
coupon

il **caffè** coffee
caldo/a hot
il **Cambio** Exchange
Bureau
la **camera** room
il **campeggio** camp-site
capisco I understand
il **cappuccino** frothy milky
coffee
caro/a dear, expensive
la **carta** card
carta carburante
fuel token card
carta di credito
credit card
la **cartolina** postcard
la **cassa** cash desk
c'è there is
cento hundred
il **centro** centre;
centro storico historic
centre
che? what?
che cosa? what?
chiamo: mi chiamo I
am called;
come si chiama? what's
your name?

la chiave key
il chilo kilogramme
chiuso/a closed;
ci there; **ci sono** there are
ciao hi there, see you
la cioccolata chocolate
la città city, town
la coincidenza connection
il colore colour
come? how? what?
come like, such as
completo/a full (of a hotel etc.)
compreso/a included; **tutto compreso** all inclusive
con with
il conto bill, account
il contorno vegetable
controllare to check
il coperto cover charge
il corso wide street
la cosa thing; **che cosa?** what?
così like this, like that
costare to cost; **quanto costa?** How much does it cost?
la cotoletta cutlet
cotto/a cooked
crudo/a raw

da from
dal tabaccaio at the tobacconist's
davanti in front of
del, della, dell' of the
dentro inside
il dépliant brochure
desidera? what would you like?
destra right
a destra on the right
deve you must
di of

dica tell me
dietro behind
il diretto a fast train
dispiace: mi dispiace I am sorry
la doccia shower
dolce mild, sweet
domani tomorrow
la doppia double room
dove where; **dov'è?** where is?
dritto straight on

e and
è is
ecco here is, here are
l' edicola (f) newspaper kiosk
esatto exactly
l' espresso (m) coffee, express train
l' etto (m) 100 grams

facciamo we make, we do; let's make (it), let's do (it)
la farmacia chemist's shop
fare to do, to make
il favore favour; **per favore** please
feriale: giorni feriali working days
la fermata bus-stop
la festa festival
festivo: giorni festivi Sundays and holidays
la fetta slice
la figlia daughter
il figlio son
i figli children
il filobus trolley
fino a as far as
fondo: in fondo at the back, in the end

il **formaggio** cheese
fra between; **fra dieci minuti** in ten minutes' time
la **fragola** strawberry
francese French
il **francobollo** stamp
il **fratello** brother
freddo/a cold
la **frutta** fruit

il **Galles** Wales
gallese Welsh
il **gasolio** diesel fuel
gassato/a fizzy
la **gassosa** fizzy lemonade
il **gelato** ice cream
la **giacca** jacket
il **giorno** day
la **gita** trip
la **gomma** tyre
grande big
la **granita** crushed ice drink
la **Gran Bretagna** Great Britain
grazie thanks
guardi! look!
guasto/a broken (down)

importante important
l' **indirizzo** (m) address
l' **Inghilterra** (f) England
inglese English
l' **insalata** (f) salad
insegnare to teach
l' **Irlanda** (f) Ireland
irlandese Irish
l' **isola** (f) island
l' **Italia** (f) Italy
italiano/a Italian

laggiù down there
il **lago** lake
lasciare to leave
ho lasciato I have left

il **latte** milk
la **lattina** tin, can
il **lavoro** work; **lavoro** I work
lentamente slowly
il **lettino** sun-lounger, little bed
lì there
libero/a free
il **limone** lemon
il **listino** short list
il **litro** litre
lontano/a far

ma but
la **macchina** machine, car;
la **macchina fotografica** camera
la **macelleria** butcher's shop
male bad, badly
il **mare** sea
il **marito** husband
maturo/a ripe
la **mela** apple
mezzo/a half
la **mezz'ora** half an hour
mille thousand
mio my; **il mio** mine
misto mixed
la **moglie** wife
molto much, many
la **moneta** change, coin

nero black
niente nothing
di niente don't mention it; **nient' altro** nothing else?
la **nocciola** hazel-nut
il **nome** name
il **normale** 2-star petrol
la **notte** night
il **numero** number
il **nuoto** swimming

oggi today
ogni every
ogni due ore every two hours
l' **olio** (m) oil
l' **ombrellone** (m) sunshade
l' **ora** (f) hour, time
l' **orario** (m) time-table

il **pane** bread
il **panino** bread roll
la **paninoteca** sandwich bar
parlare to speak
Partenze Departures
partire to leave;
  a che ora parte? what time does it leave?
le **patate fritte** chips
la **patente (di guida)** driving licence
peccato pity
il **pedalo** pedal boat
la **pensione** boarding house
la **pera** pear
permesso excuse me
perso lost
la **pesca** peach, fishing
il **pezzo** piece, bit
il **piacere** pleasure;
  per piacere please;
  mi piace I like
il **piano** storey;
  al piano terreno on the ground floor
la **pianta** map
la **piazza** square
piccolo/a little
pieno/a full
pistacchio pistachio
più more; **un po' di più** a bit more
un **po' (di)** a bit (of)
un **pochino** a tiny bit
poi then

il **pomodoro** tomato
la **porchetta** roast suckling pig
il **portafoglio** wallet
posso I can
la **posta** post-office
il **posto** place
prego please, don't mention it
prendere to take;
  prendo I take;
  prendete? will you have?
la **prenotazione** reservation
primo first;
  il primo first course
il **progetto** plan, project
la **promozione** promotion, special offer
pronto ready, immediately, 'hello' on the telephone
il **Pronto Soccorso** casualty department
il **prosciutto** ham
prossimo/a next
provare to try
pulito clean
il **pullman** coach, bus
può he/she can, you (**lei**) can

qua here
quale? which?
quanto/a how much?
  per quanto tempo? for how long?
quanti/e? how many?
quattro four
questo/a this

la **ragazza** girl
il **ragazzo** boy
il **ragù** meaty sauce
il **ridotto** reduced fare ticket

riparare to repair
il **ristorante** restaurant
il **ritorno** return
rosso/a red
la **roulotte** caravan

lo **scatto** unit of payment (on telephone)
lo **sconto** discount
lo **scontrino** receipt
scozzese Scottish
la **Scozia** Scotland
la **sdraia** deckchair (also **lo** or **la sdraio**)
secondo/a second;
   il **secondo** second course
il **semaforo** traffic lights
sempre always
la **serratura** lock
la **settimana** week
si one (in general sense)
sì yes
signori sir and madam
la **singola** single room
sinistra left; **a sinistra** on the left
il **sole** sun
solo only, alone
soltanto only
sono I am
la **sorella** sister
la **spiaggia** beach
stare to feel, to stay
la **strada** street, road
subito immediately
suo/a his, her, your
il **super** 4-star petrol
il **supermercato** supermarket

la **tabaccheria** tobacconist's shop
la **taglia** size
il **tavolo** table

il **té** tea
tedesco/a German
il **tempo** time;
   per quanto tempo? for how long?
la **tenda** tent
terzo/a third
il **toast** toasted sandwich
la **toilette** toilet
tornare to return;
   torni come back
tra between, in;
   tra un'ora in an hour's time
il **traghetto** ferry
il **treno** train
troppo too, too much
trovare to find;
   si trova it is situated
il **turismo** tourism
turistico/a tourist;
   il menu turistico basic set menu
tutto all
   tutti everyone
   tutti(e) e due both

l' **ufficio** office
ultimo/a last
l' **uva** grapes

va go; **va bene** okay
la **vacanza** holiday
vedere to see;
   vediamo un po let's have a look
verde green
la **via** street
vicino near
il **vigile** policeman
il **vino** wine
la **vongola** cockle
vorrei I would like
vuole? Do you want?